Emma,

Enjoy my first children's book.

Crystal

Along Came a Little...

by Crystal Albright

ISBN: 978-1-7343636-1-6 (Paperback)

ISBN: 978-1-7343636-0-9 (Hardback)

Published by UBuildABook, LLC. 2020, in the United States of America.

Book design by © Bethany Kerr

Illustrations by © Bethany Kerr

First printing edition 2020 albrightsmiles.com

This story is dedicated to my grandparents, O'neal and Eunice Shelton, who gave me unconditional love, a home- as long as they were here- and always reminded me to slow down to enjoy the little things. They loved children more than anything or anyone and would love to read this story to my sweet boys today.

A huge thanks to my illustrator and editor, Bethany Kerr, who inspires beauty all around her with unbelievable talent and hidden strength. Without her uncanny ability to create while I jumble through my ADD brain of ideas, this never would have happened. I look forward to watching her fly even higher in her art career!

This book has been on my bucket list for many years. Panama City Beach is my forever home now with beauty that both calms and inspires me. Don't let a summer pass without putting your toes in the sand, swimming in the saltwater, and making memories with the precious time and people you have.

1 giant sandcastle

sitting on the shore...

5

Along came a little boy

it was no more.

2 snappy crabs

happy, warm, and wet...

9

Along came a little boy

crabs scooped in a net.

11

3 bright umbrellas

Along came a little boy

Now mommy has to mend.

4 tiny seashells

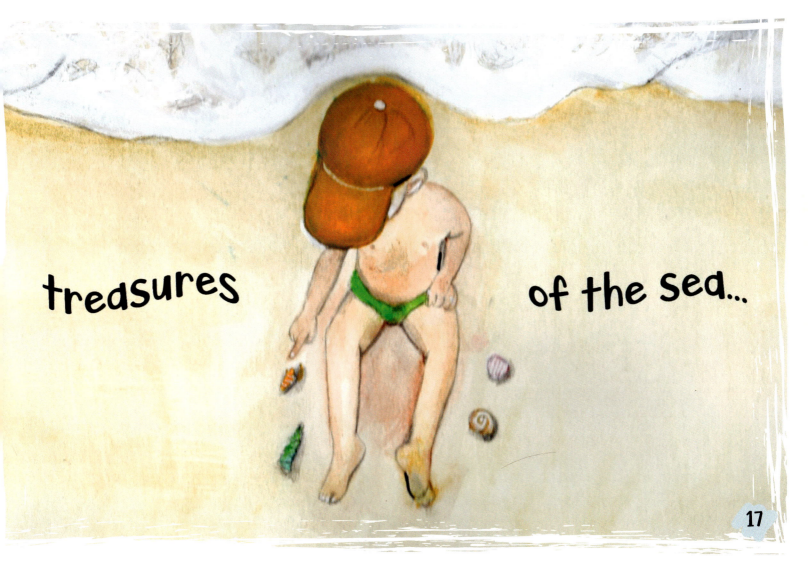

treasures

of the sea...

Along came a little boy

Shells tossed with glee

19

5 noisy seagulls

soaring in the sky...

21

Along came a little boy

chasing birds, arms a fly

23

 **colorful shovels**

scattered in the sand...

25

Along came a little boy

shovel swords in hand.

7 drops of water

falling from the sky...

29

Along came a little boy

jumping puddles oh so high.

8 new friends

playing by the shore...

Along came a little boy

Showing how he adores.

9 dolphins dancing

splashing in the waves

Along came a little boy

sweet memories to save

39

 **colorful coquinas**

burrowing down below

Along came a little boy

feet changing

water flow

43

All the days of summer

remembered through the year...

That little boy who came along

grows fast while mommy holds dear

Meet the Author

Crystal Albright is a mother to two dynamic boys, serial entrepreneur, chocolate lover, realtor, and beach obsessed writer living in paradise in Panama City Beach, Florida. She is an avid photographer, dive master, and once won the Cullman County Fair blue ribbon for her no bake cookies. It may or may not be the last time she baked.

Raised as the oldest of 7 children in Cullman, Al. she met Bethany Kerr at the age of 14. 25 years later they began collaborating on what would become a series of children's books and art designs to launch into the next grand adventure!

Meet the Illustrator

Bethany Kerr is a mother to 8 children, an artist, illustrator & art instructor in Cullman, Alabama. She has painted murals for the city of Cullman, Al., is a book author and has illustrated 7 books, teaches art at Fairview Elementary School, and has a blog with art tutorials at **icandrawnow.com**.

You can see and shop her watercolor paintings or request a commission piece on her etsy shop at: **etsy.com/shop/bethanykerrfineart**